A LITTLE

SZECHUAN

COOKBOOK

TERRY TAN

Illustrated by SHERRI TAY

CHRONICLE BOOKS

SAN FRANCISCO

First published in 1995 by
The Appletree Press Ltd, 19–21 Alfred Street,
Belfast BT2 8DL
Tel. +44 (0) 1232 243074
Fax +44 (0) 1232 246756

A Little Szechuan Cookbook

First published in the United States in 1995
by Chronicle Books, 275 Fifth Street,
San Francisco, CA 94103

ISBN 0-8118-1152-2

9 8 7 6 5 4 3 2 1

A note on measures

Spoon measurements are level except where otherwise
indicated. Seasonings, especially chilies and peppercorns,
can be adjusted to taste. Recipes serve four. In a
Szechuan meal, individual dishes are rarely, if ever,
prepared to serve everyone at the table. Meals always
consist of several dishes which are shared as the meal
progresses.

Introduction

It is often said that the fire in Szechuan cuisine evolved to counteract the *chang chi* (jungle dampness) of the province's sultry, hot summers. But the culinary heritage is much more than hot chili pods *per se*. The mountain-ringed Red Basin in western China is blessed with fertile soil watered by an irrigation system laid down 2,000 years ago to supplement water from the four tributaries (*szechuan*) of the Yangtze River. Riverine and land fecundity are manifested in multiple crops of rice, corn, millet potatoes, beans, peas, and bamboo. There's abundant game, chickens, pigs, and oxen. Szechuan cooking owes its characteristic spicy flavors to Buddhist missionaries who made their way to the province from Burma, Thailand and India in the first century A.D. They also implanted their influences in the southern neighboring province of Yunnan, bringing and cultivating numerous spices and herbs that laid a spicy aromatic culinary foundation.

Cooking techniques in Szechuan are remarkable for their preservative promise; salted, dried, smoked, pickled, and spiced meats, seafood, and vegetables are lavished with the prized Szechuan chili peppers and peppercorns. Garlic, ginger, and onions also figure dominantly, creating a delicious amalgam of salty, sour, bitter, fragrant, and spicy flavors. Tea leaves and camphor wood are used to smoke meats. Nature has worked on a grand scale in Szechuan shaping the landscape amid winding rows of rice terraces, providing the blessing of an eleven-month growing season to create one of the most distinctive cuisines in the world. Many Szechuan dishes have become universally known – hot-and-sour soup, sweet corn soup, and chicken and chili peppers, just to name a few.

The Szechuan Kitchen

As one of China's regional cuisines, Szechuan cooking naturally revolves around most of the ingredients in the Chinese spectrum but its evolution is based largely on fiery and pungent chilies and peppercorns. Utensils remain classic as in any other Chinese kitchen, based on the "Holy Trinity" of wok, chopping board, and heavy cleaver. All else can be found in any western kitchen.

Bamboo Shoots Canned or fresh, they must be soaked or blanched before cooking.

Beancurd (Tofu) Preserved, fresh, or dried, it is fundamental to Szechuan cooking, complementing and absorbing just about every flavor.

Beancurd (fermented) Canned, red, or white and very pungent. To be used sparingly as a marinade or stir-fry seasoning.

Chili Peppers Dried pods of varying sizes, usually cooked whole and packing a terrific wallop.

Chili Sauce Any commercial chili sauce or Tabasco sauce can be used where indicated.

Chinese Wine Of they many types used, Hua Teow or Kaoliang are best for Szechuan dishes. Alternative: sherry.

Chinese Parsley Larger leaf than coriander and similar to celery in flavor.

Dried Mushroom These have to be soaked until soft and cooked whole or sliced.

Garlic Used liberally, sometimes half a dozen cloves or more per dish, usually in tandem with ginger root.

Ginger Root Used grated, sliced, or puréed and compatible with garlic and onions.

Green onion Chopped for garnish or sliced with stir-fried chicken and meat.

Hoi Sin Sauce Thick, sweet bean paste used as marinade or stir-fry sauce.

Hot Soy Bean Paste Also called Dou Ban Chiang, used much like yellow bean or *hoi sin* sauce.

Maltose Chinese honey used for glazing poultry and as a sweetener.

Sesame Oil An aromatic, nutty oil used as a seasoning and not a cooking agent.

Sesame Paste A nutty, oily paste not unlike peanut butter, used to thicken sauces.

Salted Black Beans Pungent, dry black beans that can be added to stir-fries in place of salt.

Shallots Small, red onions that are sweeter and more fragrant than large yellow ones.

Soy Sauce Dark or light, a fundamental in all Chinese cooking.

Szechuan Peppercorns (Fagara) Smaller and hotter than normal peppercorns with a distinct aniseed flavor.

Szechuan Preserved Vegetable (Kohlrabi) Sold in vacuum packs or cans, essential to soups and stir-fries.

Wood Ears Also known as Tree Ears, a dry fungus to be soaked before stir-frying or adding to soups.

Flavors and Methods

Szechuan cuisine is based on the culinary structure of flavors (imparted to food during cooking or by means of a sauce) and methods. The flavors are:

Tien – sweet from sugar or honey
Xien – salty from soy sauce or salt
Suan – sour from rice vinegar
Ku – bitter from green onion or leek
Xiang – fragrant from garlic or ginger root
Ma – nutty from sesame or other oil seeds
La – hot from chili peppers or peppercorns

The eight methods are:

Hang-yu Refers to a master sauce made from chili oil, sugar, green onion, ginger root, garlic, sesame seed paste, and soy sauce and poured over a dish just before serving.

Tiao-ma Szechuan peppercorns and sesame seed paste are predominant here with the addition of soy sauce, ginger root, sugar, and green onion. Poured over a dish before serving.

Ma-la A fiery basis of chili peppers and peppercorns with ginger root, green onion, soy sauce, and sugar imparting a glossy brown color to food.

Guai-wei A sweet, sour, hot, and spicy blend with no single predominant flavor from peppercorns, sesame oil, sesame paste, garlic, green onion, vinegar, sugar, chili oil, and soy sauce.

Tiang-zu A sauce containing ginger root, soy sauce, vinegar, and sesame oil and eaten cold.

Gan-chao Literally "dry fried", using little or no oil over a high heat, resulting in crispy and deeply-colored vegetables.

Yu-xiang Stir or deep-frying and then cooking further with liberal amounts of chopped garlic, ginger root, hot bean paste, and spices.

Szechuan Hot and Sour Soup

A standard starter soup in most Chinese restaurants, it lends itself to much ingenuity though the basic seasoning remains the same. To it can be added chicken, pork, seafood, or it can simply be left as a light, clear but spicy vegetable-based soup.

---

8 oz pork, chicken, or prawns, diced
5 cups water or stock
³/₄ cup Szechuan preserved vegetable, chopped
1 egg white, lightly beaten
1 tsp cornstarch, dissolved in a little water
2 whole fresh, red chilies, finely chopped
1 stalk green onion, finely chopped
1 tsp ground black pepper
2 tbsp sesame oil
shallot to garnish

Combine meat, water, and vegetable in a pot and bring to a boil. Cook for 15 minutes and add all other ingredients. When soup is slightly thickened, remove from heat and serve immediately, garnished with more chopped green onion or fried shallots.

Chicken and Sweet Corn Soup

This is a universally loved soup and uniquely Szechuan in evolution. Do not use corn niblets in place of creamed corn as they do not give the characteristic sweet flavor, or the creamy texture essential to this dish. Chinese restaurants have a tendency to use cornstarch to thicken the soup, which makes it congeal. Egg does this better and you get a nice mix of streaky egg white and yellow corn.

2¹/₂ cups water	1 egg, lightly beaten
8 oz chicken breast	2 tsp salt
1 tbsp sesame oil	1 tsp black pepper
1 can creamed corn	2 stalks green onion, chopped

In a saucepan, bring water to a boil and simmer chicken breast for about 10 minutes. Remove chicken and reserve stock. Cool and dice chicken. Put back into stock and combine with sesame oil and creamed corn. Simmer for 5 minutes and gently stir in beaten egg to thicken. Add seasoning, adjust to taste and serve with green onion sprinkled on top.

Sizzling Rice Soup

An unusual way to use rice. Szechuan chefs use leftover rice by first drying it in the sun or under a grill. This soup has its roots in peasant ingenuity but is a delicious conversation piece.

5 cups clear meat stock	2 tbsp sherry or Chinese wine
8 oz fresh prawns, shelled, and de-veined	oil for deep-frying
1¹/₂ cups mushrooms, sliced	1 cup moist cooked rice, dried into 2¹/₂ inch-diameter pieces
2 tsp salt	

Spread cooked rice, still moist, on a baking sheet or foil. Press down to make cakes and dry in a slow oven until brittle. In a large saucepan, bring stock to a boil and add prawns, mushrooms, seasoning, and sherry. Simmer for five minutes and pour into a

soup tureen to keep hot while you prepare the rice. In a wok, heat oil until smoking and deep-fry rice pieces until crisp and light brown. Drain and arrange in individual soup bowls (about six). To serve, pour hot stock over individual bowls. The sizzling you will hear gives the soup its name.

Pickled Salad

This is an unusual starter salad, a Szechuan version of a classic salad with vinaigrette dressing (Szechuan Peppercorn Sauce, see p. 16). Requiring very little time to prepare, it is wonderful as a summer salad, especially with barbecued and grilled meats. The salting is essential to retain crispness in the vegetables.

1 whole cucumber, peeled, and cored	1 tsp sugar
2 tsp salt	1 tbsp light soy sauce
1 lb white cabbage, cored, and finely shredded	2 tbsp sesame oil
1 tsp garlic, crushed	2 tbsp wine vinegar
1 tsp Szechuan peppercorns, ground	2 tbsp sesame seeds
	Chinese parsley to garnish

Slice cucumber into diamond shapes and sprinkle lightly with salt. Leave for at least an hour together with shredded cabbage. Squeeze out moisture, a few handfuls at a time, and dry further on paper towels. Mix garlic, peppercorns, sugar, soy sauce, sesame oil, and vinegar in a bottle, shake well, and chill. To serve, spread vegetables on a large cabbage or lettuce leaf and pour dressing all over. Sprinkle with sesame seeds and top with a sprig of Chinese parsley.

Szechuan Peppercorn Sauce

Most of the sauces used in Szechuan cooking are available commercially but this one is a master blend that most chefs will make themselves. Based on the *tiang-zu* cold sauce method (see p. 8), it is ideal with salads or poured over plain meats and seafood.

Szechuan peppercorns are the dried berries of a citrus family shrub.

4 tsp Szechuan peppercorns	4 tbsp sesame oil
4 stalks green onion, chopped	3 tbsp hot water
2 tbsp ginger root, finely grated	3 tbsp wine vinegar
2 tsp salt	1 tbsp sugar
4 tbsp soy sauce	

Crush the peppercorns very finely and mix well with other ingredients. Chill, and serve with salad or cold meat.

Prawns on Toast

As ubiquitous as the western shrimp cocktail, this appetizer has probably seen more interpretations than a star-gazer's zodiac. It is actually the simplest thing to make, requiring no more than good, fresh prawns, a little minced pork, bread, and sesame seeds. A good way to use up less-than-fresh bread.

8 slices white bread, crusts removed	1 tsp salt
	1/2 tsp black pepper
4 oz minced pork	1 egg, lightly beaten
8 oz minced prawns	2 tbsp sesame seeds
1 tbsp sesame oil	oil for deep frying

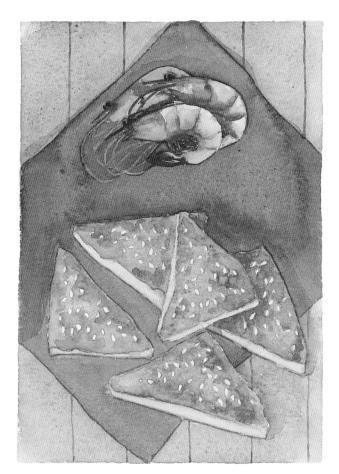

Cut each slice of bread into two triangles. Combine pork, prawns, sesame oil, and seasoning and mix well. Brush each triangle of bread with beaten egg and spread about 1 level tablespoon of mixture on it, pressing down firmly. Sprinkle sesame seeds on top, pressing down lightly. When all are done, heat oil in a skillet until smoking and deep-fry a few at a time until golden brown. Drain on paper towels and serve with sliced cucumber and chili sauce.

Poached Kidneys in Hot Sauce

Kidneys are a delicacy in China and are usually scored before cooking to expose the maximum surface area. When cooked, each kidney curls up to resemble a *hua* (flower), symbolizing prosperity, hence the many Chinese dishes that begin with *hua*. This dish can be served as a main course or – believe it or not – as a breakfast item. The sauce is a variation of the Szechuan *Tiao-ma* (see p. 8) blend.

12 oz pig's kidneys	1 tbsp wine vinegar
2 tsp salt	1 tbsp chili oil (available in
1 whole cucumber, sliced	Chinese grocery stores)
1 tbsp sesame seed paste	1 tbsp ginger root, finely grated
(available in Chinese	1 clove garlic, minced
grocery stores)	1 tsp Szechuan peppercorns,
3 tbsp water	crushed
2 tbsp soy sauce	

Clean and halve the kidneys. Remove all white membrane. Cut each into thick slices and score each deeply in a criss-cross pattern. Sprinkle with salt and leave aside for a few minutes. Sprinkle salt on sliced cucumber and leave aside for 15 minutes, then squeeze out all moisture. Blend sesame seed paste, water, and all seasoning ingredients into a thick paste. Blanch kidneys in a large pot of boiling water until they curl up and are cooked through. Arrange cucumber on a plate. Toss kidneys in paste and arrange on cucumber slices. The dish can be served hot or cold.

Braised Carp in Hot Bean Sauce

The tributaries of the Yangtze abound with carp, but any rich, oily fish such as herring, mackerel, or snapper will do. Cod, skate, and halibut will give good results but lack the fulsome flavor.

---

1 lb carp or other fish, whole or filleted	3 tbsp Szechuan hot bean paste (available in Chinese grocery stores)
1 tbsp soy sauce	
oil for deep frying	2 tbsp Chinese wine or sherry
3 tbsp oil for stir fry	1 tsp sugar
2 stalks green onion, chopped	1 tbsp chili sauce
1 tbsp ginger root, finely chopped	2 tbsp sesame oil
1 clove garlic, minced	2 tbsp wine vinegar
	1 cup water

If using whole fish, ask fishmonger to clean and gut but leave whole. Score across fleshy part on both sides in a criss-cross pattern. Sprinkle fish with a little soy sauce and marinate for half an hour. In a wok, heat enough oil to deep-fry fish. Fry until crisp and set aside. Heat 3 tablespoons of clean oil in wok and fry green onion, ginger, and garlic until light brown. Stir in bean paste, sherry, sugar, chili sauce, sesame oil, vinegar, and water. Simmer over medium

heat until sauce is slightly thick and glossy. Add fish and cook it for 5 minutes further to heat. Garnish with chopped green onion.

Tea-Smoked Fish Slices

Regional cuisines cross over frequently in China and, while this dish hails from the eastern seaboard, smoking with tea leaves is an authentic Szechuan cooking technique. This is a delicious way to smoke fish.

2 tbsp jasmine tea leaves	2 tbsp ginger root, chopped
5 tbsp raw rice or barley grains	I tsp sugar
I lb cod, sliced	I tsp Szechuan peppercorns
Marinade:	pinch of 5-spice powder
3 tbsp Chinese wine or sherry	(available in Chinese
2 tbsp dark soy sauce	grocery stores)
2 tbsp green onion, chopped	

Mix together marinade ingredients and marinate fish for a few hours or overnight in the refrigerator. Drain well. Mix the tea leaves and rice or barley and place on a double layer of foil in a dry, clean wok. Lightly oil the bamboo slats of a steamer so fish will not stick. Place fish directly into the steamer and cover tightly, winding a length of towel around the lid for extra insulation. Place steamer in wok, turn heat on medium and "smoke" for half an hour or more until fish is done and smells aromatic. Do not use too high a heat or rice and tea will char too fast giving a burnt smell rather than a smoked one.

Shrimp Fu Yung

Fu Yung always refers to the use of egg in any dish, though it is usually combined with shrimps, prawns, or scallops, or used as a filling with steamed bread or lettuce leaves. *Fu Yung* is indigenous to practically all regional Chinese cooking. Never use cooked shellfish for this dish as it will become overdone and tough.

---

4 eggs
1 tsp cornstarch blended with 2 tbsp water
8 oz fresh prawns, shelled, and de-veined
1 tbsp Chinese wine or dry sherry
1 tsp salt
1/2 tsp black pepper
2 stalks green onion, chopped
2 tbsp garden peas
4 tbsp baked ham, chopped
5 tbsp vegetable oil

In a medium-sized bowl, beat eggs lightly, add salt, pepper, wine, and stir in cornstarch mixture. This is the secret to making mixtures smooth and moist. Heat oil in a wok and pour in egg, swirling it around a little. When egg is half-cooked, heap prawns, green onion, ham, and peas on egg and stir around a little. Cook until egg is nearly set and fold over to make a half-moon shape. Cook on one side for a few moments, then flip over carefully and cook until brown edges appear. Lift from wok and serve hot. You can also stir the egg and filling together and cook it as a "loose" *Fu Yung*.

Pepper Prawns

A classic Szechuan dish incorporating hot, sweet, and salty flavors with a liberal dash of chili sauce – the *guai-wei* sauce. Tiger prawns are best for this imperial dish. This dish has also spawned many similar concoctions in Southeast Asia, notably Singapore Chili Prawns.

---

12 prawns, heads removed but shell left on
1 tbsp soy sauce
2 tbsp Chinese wine or dry sherry
1 tsp salt
1 tsp Szechuan peppercorns, crushed
1 tsp sugar
1 tsp garlic purée
1 tbsp chili sauce or 2 tsp Tabasco
2 stalks green onion, chopped
1 tbsp ginger root, ground
4 tbsp oil
parsley to garnish

Marinate prawns in wine and soy sauce for half an hour. Heat oil and fry garlic purée until fragrant, then add prawns (but not the marinade), salt, peppercorns, sugar, garlic, chili sauce, green onion, ginger, and oil. Stir over high heat until prawns turn pink – about 5 minutes. Add marinade and stir until sauce is fully blended. Serve garnished with parsley sprigs.

Deep-Fried Spiced Fish

With a whole fish scored and bathed in hot sauce, this makes a grand presentation, especially for festive occasions. Ideal fish to use are whole mullet, bream, bass, or grouper. Fish fillets, however, are much easier to handle and fry, unless you have a very large wok.

---

1 whole fish, weighing about 1 1/2 lb, or 1 1/2 lb fish fillets
1 tbsp fresh ginger root, ground
2 stalks green onion, chopped
1 tsp Szechuan peppercorns, crushed finely
2 tbsp Chinese wine or red wine vinegar
1 tsp sugar
1 tbsp soy sauce
4 tbsp sesame oil
oil for deep-frying

If using whole fish, clean and gut it. Make several diagonal cuts across both sides of body and marinate in ginger, green onion, peppercorns, wine, sugar, and soy sauce for at least half an hour. Drain and pat dry. In a large wok, deep fry until crisp. Remove and keep warm. Blend the sesame oil with marinade and bring to a gentle boil. Pour over fish and serve with slices of lemon.

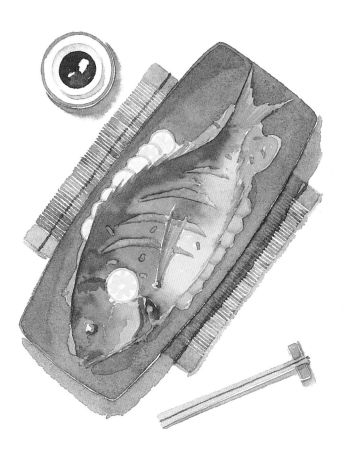

Fried Chili Pork

Though chilies are a mainstay in Szechuan cooking, restaurants in China do not offer side plates of either fresh cut chilies or chili sauce, as they do in the west. The fire is infused in the dish. This is a classic recipe using the *Ma-la* sauce (see p. 8) from the provincial capital of Chengdu, regarded as the culinary epicenter of Szechuan.

---

2 tbsp light soy sauce
1 tbsp dry sherry
1 tsp cornstarch
8 oz pork fillet, cut into 2-inch strips
1 tbsp Szechuan hot chili bean paste
$^1/_2$ tsp black pepper
1 tsp sugar
2 tbsp red wine vinegar
4 tbsp oil
1 tbsp ginger root, ground
2 tsp crushed garlic
1 cup bamboo shoots, sliced
5 dried Chinese mushrooms, soaked until soft
green onion to garnish

Mix soy sauce, sherry, and cornstarch and marinate pork for 15 minutes. Mix the chili bean paste with pepper, sugar, and vinegar. In a wok, heat oil and fry garlic and ginger until light brown. Lift pork strips from marinade and add to wok. Stir over high heat for a few minutes and add bamboo shoots and mushrooms. Stir over medium heat for 2 minutes and add all other ingredients and bring to a quick boil. Add marinade and remove from heat when mixture thickens. Serve garnished with chopped green onion.

Yunnan Roast Duck

Yunnan cuisine originates to the south of the Szechuan province but the two traditions share the same spicy roots. In fact, most Szechuan restaurants will have a fair number of Yunnan dishes and it's hard to tell the difference between the two cuisines. (Yunnan is also famous for its black *Pu-er* tea and ham.) Traditionally, a very young duckling is used for this dish and is roasted on a pine-needle fire. You can make do with the simple option of a good duckling and a convection oven. The recipe is simplicity itself, though the duck must be dried overnight.

---

1 oven-ready duckling (4–5 lb)
2 tbsp honey
5 stalks green onion, shredded
1/2 cucumber, cored and shredded
mandarin pancakes (available in Chinese grocery stores)
hoi sin sauce (available in Chinese grocery stores)

Boil a large pot of water and scald the duck quickly. Drain the duck and wipe dry. Brush honey liberally all over duck while it is still warm from the scalding. Using a meat hook, hang the duck in a dry place (or out in the sun on your laundry line!) for about 12 hours.

Pre-heat oven to 450°F. Place duck in a roasting pan and roast for 45 to 60 minutes, turning once halfway through. Allow to cool for an hour before serving with mandarin pancakes. These can be bought frozen in most Chinese grocery stores and need only to be steamed for 5 minutes (or microwaved for 20 seconds each). To eat, rub each pancake with *hoi sin* sauce, then top with shredded green onion, cucumber, and a piece or two of duck meat with the

crispy skin. There will be quite a lot of pink meat left over. Strip it off and use for another stir-fry dish such as Duck with Almonds (see below). The carcass may be boiled down for rich stock.

Duck with Almonds

This is a marvelous way of using up leftover duck meat from an earlier roast. As it is already partially cooked, you cut down on cooking time.

---

2 tbsp oil
1 tbsp ginger root, shredded
12 oz duck meat, shredded
2 tbsp soy sauce
2 stalks green onion, chopped
1 tsp salt
3 tbsp Chinese wine or sherry
1 tsp cornstarch dissolved in 3 tbsp water
5 tbsp water
4 tbsp split almonds
watercress to garnish

Heat oil in a wok or skillet and fry ginger for 2 minutes. Add duck, soy sauce, green onion, and salt and stir over high heat for 1 minute. Add wine, cornstarch mixture, and water and bring to a quick boil to thicken the sauce. Just before serving, toss in almonds and mix well before serving garnished with sprigs of watercress.

Chicken with Green Peppers

This is a good stand-by dish and one that is universally cooked throughout China. The Szechuan recipe calls for a little braising which results in a more moist dish. Substitute green peppers with bamboo shoots or water chestnuts, if you prefer, as the basic flavors remain unchanged.

---

1 lb boned, skinned chicken breast, diced
2 cloves garlic, crushed
5 tbsp water
2 tbsp light soy sauce
$1/2$ tsp pepper
2 tbsp sesame oil
1 tbsp oyster sauce or
$1/2$ a bouillon cube (dissolved in a little hot water)
2 large green peppers, diced

In a wok or skillet, heat oil and fry garlic for 1 minute until light brown. Add chicken pieces and water and braise or fry over high heat until almost dry. Add seasonings and stir rapidly to blend all flavors. Sprinkle a little more water on if mixture is too dry. Cook for 2 minutes and add diced green peppers. Toss quickly to preserve crispness of peppers, and serve hot.

Chicken and Walnuts in Hot Chili Oil

The hot *hang-yu* sauce is typical of Szechuan cuisine. Its rich red hue appeals to the eye, and the fiery sauce stimulates the taste buds. Most Chinese grocery stores sell different versions of chili oil. Look for the type that is pure filtered oil rather than that cluttered with ground chili residue.

1 1/2 lb chicken breast, boned, and skinned	**Sauce:**
2 stalks green onion	1/2 onion, finely chopped
1 tbsp ginger root, ground	2 tbsp soy sauce
oil for deep-frying	2 tbsp hot chili oil (available in Chinese grocery stores)
1 1/2 cups walnuts, shelled	2 tbsp sesame oil
coriander to garnish	1 tsp Szechuan peppercorns, finely ground
	1 tsp sugar
	1 tsp cornstarch

Dice chicken into 1/2-inch chunks and place in a large pot with green onion and ginger. Add just enough water to cover. Bring to a boil and simmer for 15 minutes until chicken is opaque. Don't overcook or chunks will fall apart. Drain chicken and reserve stock.

Heat oil in a skillet until smoking and deep-fry walnuts quickly. Remove, drain, and cool. Blend sauce ingredients in a saucepan. Add stock to sauce and bring to a quick simmer until it thickens, then stir in chicken and walnuts. Remove from heat immediately and serve hot with a sprig of fresh coriander.

Sautéed Chicken with Onion

This may seem like a simple peasant dish but is really quite elegant in taste. Onions are used in Chinese cooking for two reasons – to sweeten the sauce and to provide the essential contrast of crispness against the softness of meat. It is important not to overcook onion as it will become mushy.

---

1 lb boned chicken, cut into bite-sized pieces
1 large onion, cut into four sections
1 tsp Szechuan peppercorns, ground
2 tbsp Chinese wine or sherry
2 tsp ginger root, ground
1 tsp salt
1 tsp sugar
2 tbsp soy sauce
5 tbsp water
2 egg whites, lightly beaten
4 tbsp oil for frying
2 tbsp sesame oil
green onion to garnish

Pat chicken pieces dry. Heat oil in a skillet and quickly fry chicken over high heat to seal in the juices. Drain chicken and reserve. Add the onion to the still smoking oil and fry for 1 minute. Add the chicken together with seasoning ingredients and water and bring to a boil. Add beaten egg white and when sauce thickens, add sesame oil to perfume the whole dish. Serve garnished with chopped green onion.

Ground Beef Omelette

An omelette takes many guises in Szechuan and Chinese cooking. Seldom, if ever, are eggs cooked alone without meat, poultry, or seafood. Nor are omelettes only meant for breakfast; they deserve a place at any meal or banquet. You can use ground beef, pork, or lamb for this dish.

---

6 eggs
2 tsp cornstarch dissolved in 3 tbsp water
1 tsp salt
5 tbsp oil
Meat filling:
4 oz ground beef
1 tsp cornstarch, dissolved in 1½ tbsp water
2 cloves garlic, crushed
1 tbsp ginger root, ground
1 tbsp Chinese wine
2 tbsp soy sauce
2 tbsp celery, chopped
green onion to garnish

Beat eggs lightly and add the cornstarch liquid and salt. This gives a smooth consistency to the omelette. Heat oil in a wok and pour in this mixture. Swirl mixture around the wok and cook until one side is done. Flip over and cook other side until just done. Remove and keep warm. Heat a little oil in the wok and fry garlic for 1 minute. Mix beef with cornstarch mixture and blend well. Add to pan together with garlic, ginger, wine, soy sauce, and celery, and stir-fry for 3 minutes until beef is done. Spread mixture over omelette and garnish with chopped green onion. You can, alternatively, cook beef mixture first and then make an omelette. When it is almost done, spread beef mixture in center and fold over to make a half-moon. Cook until egg is done and serve.

Dry-Fried Shredded Beef

This is a delicious dish often served as a filling for Szechuan pancakes, which are rather like pita bread. In fact, pita can be used as a substitute. This also makes a good topping for plain boiled rice as a kind of Chinese Beef Stroganoff, or wrapped in lettuce leaves as parcels.

---

6 tbsp oil
1 stalk celery, chopped
8 water chestnuts, diced into $1/4$ inch cubes
1 tbsp soy sauce
1 lb sirloin, shredded but not minced
2 cloves garlic, crushed
1 tbsp wine vinegar
2 tbsp sesame oil
1 tbsp Szechuan hot bean paste (available in Chinese grocery stores)
lettuce leaves or pita bread

In a wok, heat 2 tablespoons oil and fry celery and water chestnuts for 2 minutes. Add soy sauce. Remove from wok. Heat remaining oil and fry meat for 5 minutes until almost dry and dark brown. Add garlic, wine vinegar, sesame oil, and bean paste and stir for 1 minute. Add vegetables and stir well. Adjust seasoning and serve on individual lettuce leaves or inside pita bread as you please.

Szechuan Beef Steak with Snow Peas

Snow peas have only become high-profile in the past few years but deserve even more attention for their wonderful texture and sweet flavor. This vegetable holds its shape and crunch no matter how long you cook it. It figures prominently in all Chinese vegetarian cooking.

---

1 lb rump, cut into thin bite-size pieces
1 tbsp soy sauce
5 tbsp water
2 tbsp Chinese wine or sherry
1 tbsp oyster sauce (available in Chinese grocery stores)
2 cups snow peas, topped and tailed
2 tbsp oil
1 tbsp sesame oil
2 cloves garlic, sliced
1 tsp salt

Tenderize beef a bit with the blunt edge of a cleaver or mallet. Marinate in soy sauce, wine, oyster sauce, and water for 15 minutes. Prepare snow peas as above. Heat oil in a wok until smoking and add sesame oil. Put sliced garlic in to fry until light brown. Add beef pieces. Stir fry for 1 minute over high heat and add marinade and salt. Stir well to blend all flavors and adjust seasoning. Serve hot.

Double-Cooked Pork

This is a particularly delicious traditional Szechuan dish that has become very popular in countries where there are Chinese communities. The double-cooking (*yu-xiang*, see p. 8) produces a beautifully smooth texture and the complex sauce is a perfect foil for the pork fat. The normal cut used is pork belly but if the fat puts you off, use a leaner pork leg cut. The pork is sometimes deep-fried instead of boiled but that method renders it rather greasy.

---

2 lb pork belly
3 tbsp oil
1 clove garlic, crushed
4 Szechuan or ordinary dried chili peppers
1 tbsp chili sauce
1 tbsp preserved soy red bean paste (it comes in squares and is available in Chinese grocery stores)
1 tbsp hoi sin sauce (available in Chinese grocery stores)
1 tbsp tomato purée
2 tbsp Chinese wine or sherry
8 Chinese mushroom caps, soaked until soft
2 stalks green onion, chopped
fresh coriander to garnish

Place whole piece of pork in a large saucepan and cover with just enough water. Bring to a boil and simmer for 20 minutes. Leave to cool, remove pork and slice into thin pieces. (If using pork belly, leave skin on as this is what makes the dish.) Reserve stock. Heat oil in a wok and fry garlic until light brown. Add all seasoning ingredients and pork and stir for 3 to 5 minutes. Slice mushrooms into strips and add to pork together with stock and chopped green

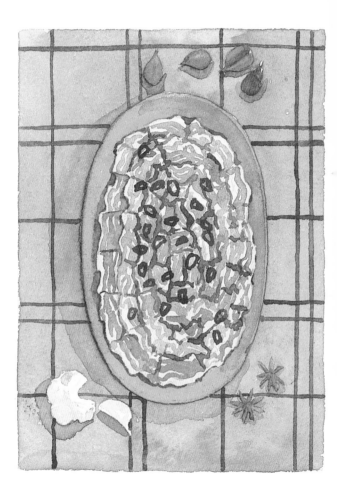

onion. Simmer until thick and gravy just coats the pork. Adjust seasoning and serve garnished with fresh coriander.

Szechuan Garlic Pork

The Chinese name for this aromatic dish is "White Cloud Pork," which alludes to the layers of fat and lean that look like cloud formations depending on your imagination. Again, the option is to substitute either leg or pork chop for pork belly but you won't get the characteristic succulence.

---

1 lb pork belly, skinned
1 tbsp ginger root, ground
2 stalks green onion, chopped
4 cloves garlic, crushed
1 tsp salt
2 tbsp soy sauce
2 star anise
2 tbsp Chinese wine or sherry
1 tbsp chili oil
1 tsp sugar
shallots or cucumber to garnish

Boil pork as for Double-Cooked Pork (see p. 48), drain and reserve stock. Cut pork into thin slices and arrange on a plate. Keep warm. Combine ginger, green onion, garlic, salt, soy sauce, star anise, wine, chili oil, and sugar in a small pot with 4–5 tablespoons of stock and bring to a simmering boil. Cook for 5 minutes over high heat to reduce. Just before serving, strain sauce over pork slices. Serve with deep-fried shallots or sliced cucumber.

Dry-Fried Bamboo Shoots

Probably one of the most versatile of all Chinese ingredients, bamboo shoots have also become widely available. They are best when young and combine well with just about anything, imparting their woody scent to any dish. This is a favorite among Buddhist vegetarians and the *gan-chao* (dry-fried) method (see p. 8)is used in many dishes.

---

2 tbsp oil
2 cloves garlic, crushed
I tbsp dried shrimp, soaked until soft, and pounded
I Szechuan dried chili pepper, soaked and chopped
I small carrot, cubed and blanched
I large can bamboo shoots, cubed
2 tbsp soy sauce
I tsp sugar
2 tbsp sesame oil
I tsp cornstarch, dissolved in 5 tbsp water

Heat oil in a wok and fry garlic for I minute. Add dried shrimp and dried chili pepper and stir for a minute. Dried shrimp soaks up oil very quickly but it will seep out again once shrimp is cooked through. Add carrot to wok with bamboo shoots, soy sauce, and sugar and continue to stir for 3 minutes. Add cornstarch liquid and sesame oil. Cook until thick, serve hot.

Dry-Fried Long Beans

This is one of my favorites and a classic Szechuan dish that makes the best use of beans. Runner, French, or any long green beans will do. The contrast in flavors and textures comes in the topping of either minced beef or pork in a rich, gingery sauce.

I lb green or French beans
oil for deep-frying
3 tbsp oil
6 oz minced beef
I tbsp ginger root, ground
2 tbsp soy sauce
4 tbsp water
I tbsp sesame oil
I tsp black pepper

Cut beans into 4-inch lengths. Heat oil in a wok and deep fry beans until they are wrinkled. Remove from wok, drain, and keep warm. Heat 3 tablespoons of oil and fry beef, ginger, and soy sauce for 3 minutes. Add water, sesame oil, and pepper, and stir over high heat until almost dry. Pile meat sauce onto beans and serve hot.

Ma-Po Bean Curd

A Szechuan import to many Chinese restaurants in the west, it combines the smooth texture of beancurd (tofu) with spicy minced pork in a delectable mix of flavors. Fresh tofu is easily available nowadays, as are long-life versions in vacuum-sealed packs.

---

1 large square tofu (about 12 oz)
2 tbsp preserved black beans
2 tbsp oil
3 stalks green onion
2 fresh chilies, chopped
1 tbsp ginger root, chopped
8 oz minced pork
2 tsp cornstarch blended with 4 tbsp water
2 tbsp Chinese wine or sherry
2 tbsp light soy sauce
1 tbsp chili sauce
2 tbsp sesame oil
1 tsp black pepper
green onion to garnish

Cut tofu into 1½-inch cubes. Scald cubes in boiling water. Drain, and place in a deep plate. Soak preserved black beans in a little hot water and mash lightly. Heat oil in a wok and fry green onion, chilies, and ginger for 2 minutes. Add pork, cornstarch mixture, and all seasoning ingredients and stir fry until pork is cooked through. Place tofu gently in mixture and toss until well blended. Alternatively, scoop mixture on tofu that has been kept warm. Serve, garnished with more chopped green onion.

Sesame Seed Cookies

As a rule, desserts are never served after a Chinese meal unless it's somebody's birthday or there is a festive reason. There are relatively few Szechuan desserts that are part of the daily meal ritual. Baking is a rarity, as ovens are scarce in China. Most sweet buns or cookies are either steamed or deep-fried. These delectable cookies are meant for snacks with tea.

2½ cups self-rising flour, sifted
¼ cup sugar
2 tbsp sesame seeds
1 tbsp vegetable or other shortening
4 tbsp water
oil for deep frying
confectioners' sugar to dust

Mix sifted flour, sugar, sesame seeds, shortening, and water and knead thoroughly until you have a soft dough that comes away from the hands. Place on a floured board and roll out to about ⅛ inch thickness. Cut into 2½-x-1-inch rectangles and make a horizontal slit in the center of each piece. Bring one end of the rectangle through the slit to form a bow-like twist. Deep-fry in a wok until golden-brown and serve, sprinkled with confectioners' sugar.

Index